ART
KEEP OUT
NO
RAISE
MOST WEDNESDAYS.
after.
Je ne sais pas.
2.
12
artifice
...BUT I LOVE YOU.
F=ma
WISE UP!
this.

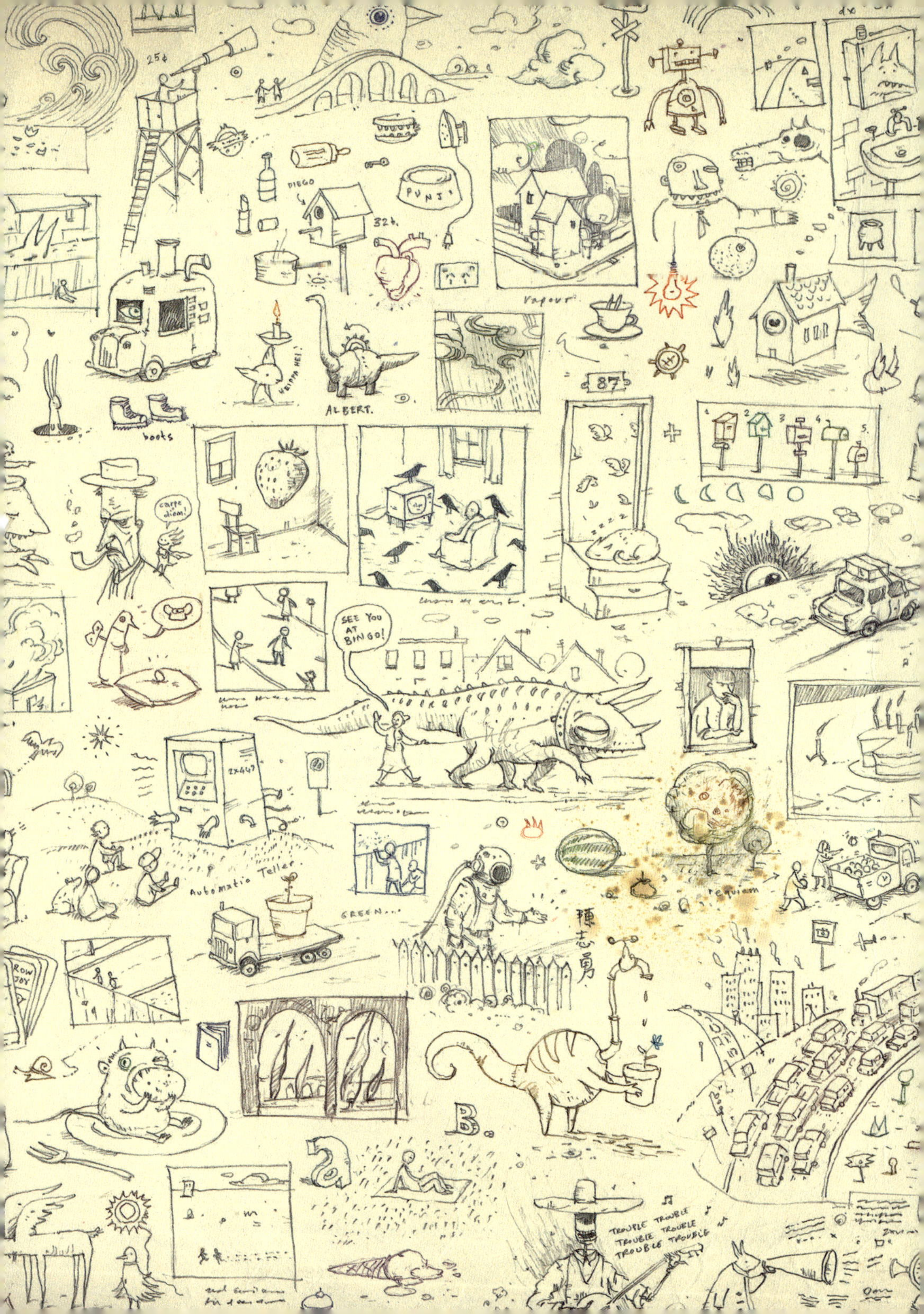

25¢
DIEGO
32¢
Vapour
HEIPPA HEI!
ALBERT.
boots
87
carpe diem!
SEE YOU AT BINGO!
2x447
Automatic Teller
GREEN...
requiem
陳志勇
B.
TROUBLE TROUBLE
TROUBLE TROUBLE
TROUBLE TROUBLE